101 SEWING SEAMS

The Most Used Seams by Fashion Designers

2nd Edition

101 Sewing Seams.
The Most Used Seams by Fashion Designers.

Copyright © 2021 by ABC Seams® Pty. Ltd.

All rights reserved. No parts of this book may be reproduced, stored in a retrieval system or transmitted, in any format or by any means, electronic, mechanical, photocopying, recording or otherwise, without the written permission of the author.

Edited and published by Memory Card Publishing.

ABC Seams® is a Trade Mark
P.O. Box 30 (4886), QLD, Australia

Email: *hello@abcseams.com*

ISBN: 978-0-6482734-6-2

Discover more at **www.abcseams.com**

ABC Seams® Team

To Marcelo, Lidia, and Oscar.

CONTENTS

Part One
INTRODUCTION
Preface 10
How to Read This Book 12
Selecting Seams 18

Part Two
SEAMS CATALOGUE
Constructions 25
Finishes 55
Details 95
Overview 108

Part Three
REFERENCE MATERIAL
Types of Stitches 112
Types of Topstitches 114
Technical Specifications 116
Index 142
Seam Codes (Index) 144
Abbreviations & Icons 146

CREDITS
About ABC Seams 149
Acknowledgments 151

Seams Catalogue

CONSTRUCTIONS

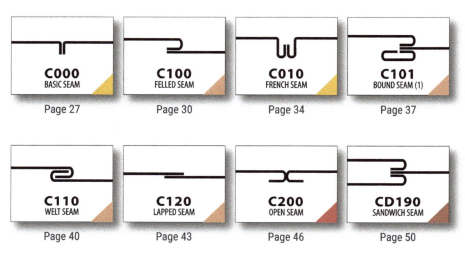

TECHNICAL SPECIFICATIONS

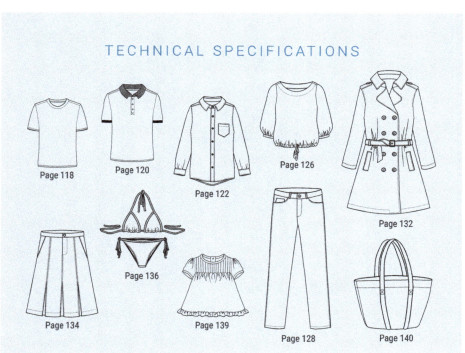

FINISHES

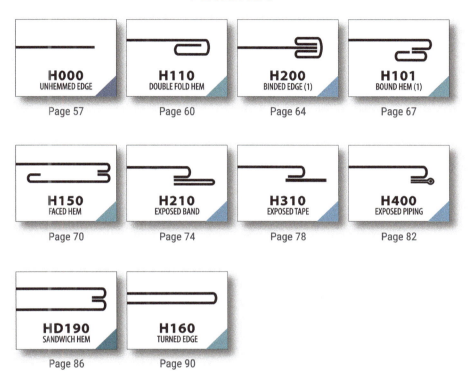

DETAILS

INTRODUCTION

Over the last few decades, the textile and apparel industry has become an extremely complex business. New fabrics every year, outsourced productions located abroad, and sophisticated logistics among different countries are just a few examples of this challenging industry.

For those of us who work with fashion, these changes directly affect the way that we work. This situation requires us to live in a constant learning process.
Nowadays, doing a good job is not enough. We must be superb, and that includes keeping ourselves up to date with the latest developments.

Having a general understanding of sewing is a crucial part of the creative process. For example, the function, the use, the aesthetic, and the cost of any textile product will affect the type of seams that we select (and vice-versa).
In addition, the wide range of stitches and seams available in the market requires a broad understanding.

That is why we have conducted detailed research identifying the currently most recognized and widely used sewing seams. The content of this book is a summary of that investigation.

Simple and Precise.

Our goal is to help make your job easier but more efficient. How? This book is a catalogue that can be used to refer to, and select, sewing seams. It will help you to be more effective by finding the specific seam you need. **You will also improve your technical knowledge which will enable you to communicate properly to achieve better results.**

Easy to Read, Easy to Use.

Whether you are a student, teacher or a professional designer, this book is for you.

Beginners will learn basic concepts, and will gain confidence and precision. Those who are more experienced will broaden their technical knowledge and will have an inspirational source to try new ideas and techniques.

HOW TO READ THIS BOOK

All sewing seams mentioned in this book are classified into three categories, depending on their main function:

1. Constructions: these are seams that join at least two layers of fabric, giving shape to the garment or product.

2. Finishes: the primary function of these seams is to prevent the fabric edge from fraying and unravelling, and at the same time providing more resistance.

3. Details: these seams embellish the design, provide volume (pleats, darts and boxes), and join pieces over the fabric (for example, patch pockets).

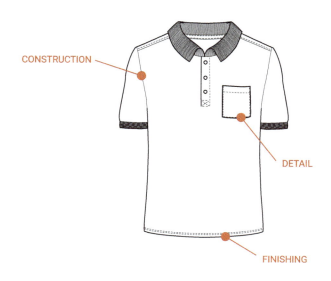

101 Sewing Seams

Each of these categories is made up of several groups of seams, and distinguish one group from another by their structure.

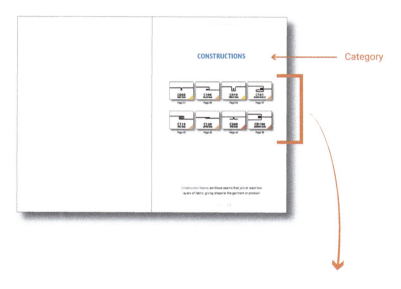

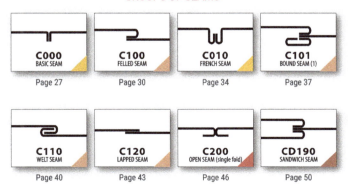

Then, each group is formed by several seams. These group of seams share the same structure, but they are sewn by different types of stitches and topstitches (p. 112 to 115).

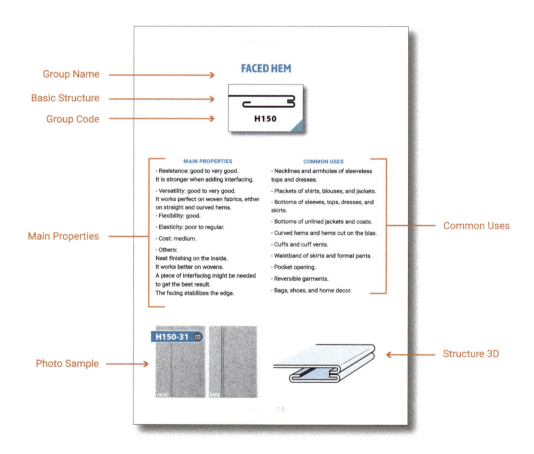

101 Sewing Seams

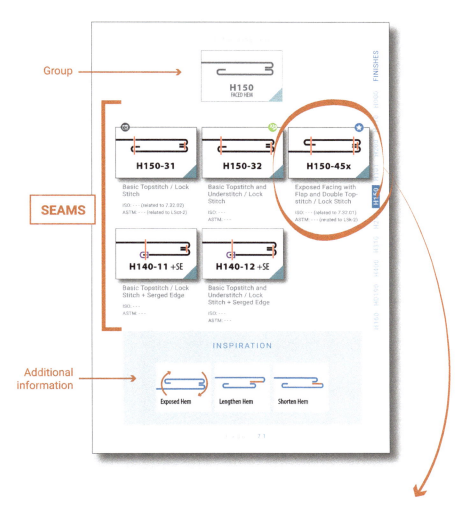

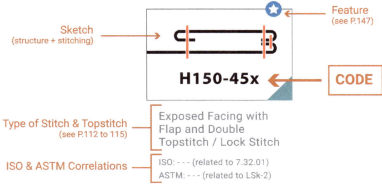

Page | 15

OVERVIEW

This chart gives you a complete view of all seams mentioned in the book. It will help you to refer, select, and compare them quickly when designing your clothing.

Note: for a large poster size of the "101 Sewing Seams OVERVIEW", visit: *www.abcseams.com/101sewingseams-overview*

SELECTING SEAMS

Initial considerations.

First of all, you need to analyze the product that you are going to develop.
You must consider the material, the use of the product, the price/cost, and all the relevant details related to the design and production. These four features are closely related to seam selection.
In case of doubt, you can use the following questions as a guide:

- *Material:* what kind of fabric is it? Is it a stretch material? Is it lightweight, medium or heavyweight? Is it a sheer fabric?

- *Use:* does it have a formal style? Is it active-wear, or will it be worn to work? Does the product need strong and resistant seams? Do the seams need to be soft and delicate?

- *Price/Cost:* who are my clients? How much will they be willing to pay for the product? How much can I afford to pay the manufacturer? Is it going to be a low-cost or an expensive garment?

- *Details:* is the product lined? Is it in contact with the skin? What type of care will it require?

Start by referring to the Overview Chart (p. 108-109) to see all the seams at once.

Step 1 – Selecting a Category

The first factor to consider is the main function of the seam: construction, finish or detail (p. 12).

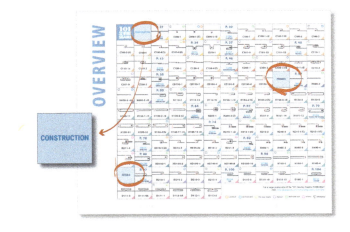

ABC Seams®

Step 2 – Selecting the Structure (or Group of Seams)

It is at this point where you need to take into account the Initial considerations (previous page).

Have a look at each seam group structure (light blue blocks) and choose the most appropriate one.

If in doubt, go to each seam group page and compare their properties to see which one is best for your design.

Step 3 – Selecting a Seam

Now it is time to think about the type of stitching and topstitching: plain stitch, overlock, cover machine, invisible stitch, etc. Besides the aesthetic aspect, consider functional characteristics, such as how strong the seams need to be, or if the garment is lined.

Step 4 – Inspiration (optional)

Some seams are widely adaptable and can be used in many ways, depending on the desired effect. To explore different options, pay attention to the Inspiration section at the end of every seam group. There you will find suggestions to try new sewing techniques.

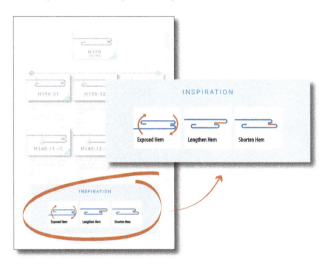

Tip: Once you have selected the seams, keep a record of them by writing down the code name on your tech pack. That information will be relevant for your manufacturer.

Note: Remember, this book includes the most popular seams in the industry – not all of them! If you need to refer to other seams, please visit the Seams Gallery on our website: *www.abcseams.com/seams-gallery*.

Part Two

SEAMS CATALOGUE

101 Sewing Seams

CONSTRUCTIONS

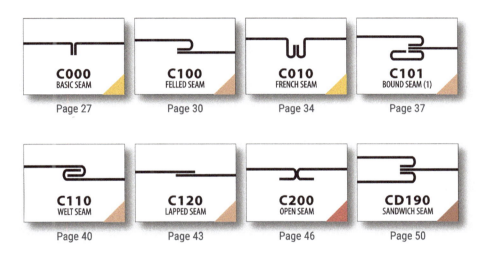

Construction Seams are those seams that join at least two layers of fabric, giving shape to the garment or product.

BASIC SEAM

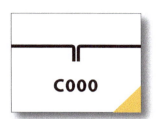

MAIN PROPERTIES

- Resistance: regular to good.
It is stronger when using an overlocker (serger): C000-1 +SE and C000-1 (OS)

- Versatility: excellent.
It is suitable for most fabrics and either on straight or curved seams.

- Flexibility: very good.

- Elasticity: good to excellent.
Good elongation recovery.

- Cost: low.
Easy and quick to make.

- Others:
No iron press required.

COMMON USES

- Side seams, mostly on casual clothing.
- Curved seams such as armholes.
- Bags and accessories.

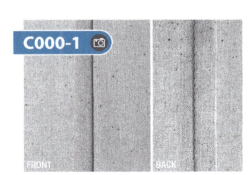

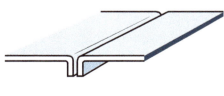

ABC Seams®

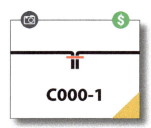  

Without Topstitch / Lock Stitch

ISO: - - - (related to 1.01.01)
ASTM: - - - (related to SSa-1)

Without Topstitch / Overlock Stitch

ISO: - - - (related to 1.01.01)
ASTM: - - - (related to SSa-1)

Without Topstitch / Lock Stitch + Serged Edge

ISO: - - - (related to 1.01.01)
ASTM: - - - (related to SSa-1)

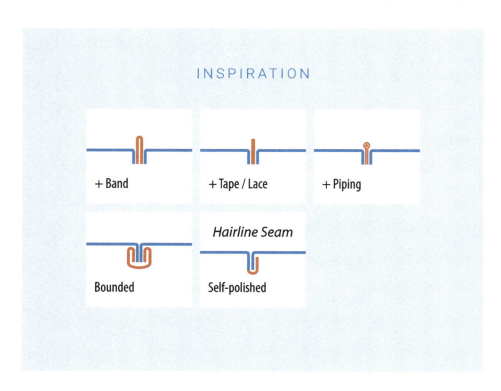

MY NOTES

MY SAMPLES

FELLED SEAM

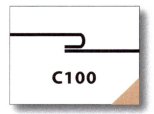

C100

MAIN PROPERTIES

- Resistance: good to very good.
It is stronger when adding a topstitch.

- Versatility: excellent.
It is suitable for any fabric (woven and knit) and either on straight or curved seams.

- Flexibility: good to very good.

- Elasticity: good to excellent.
The elasticity increases a lot when it is sewn with stretchable stitches.

- Cost: low.

- Others:
Also called "Plain Seam".

COMMON USES

- General purposes such as shoulder seam and curved seams.

- Suitable for most types of clothing and accessories.

- Lined garments and no-exposed seams or edges.

- Ready-to-wear garments.

- Sportswear.

- Children's clothing.

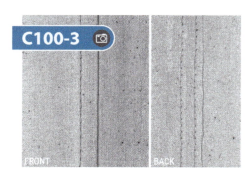

C100-3

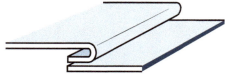

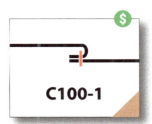

Without Topstitch / Lock Stitch

ISO: - - - (related to 1.01.01)
ASTM: - - - (related to SSa-1)

Without Topstitch / Lock Stitch + Serged Edge

ISO: - - - (related to 1.01.01)
ASTM: - - - (related to SSa-2)

Without Topstitch / Overlock Stitch

ISO: - - - (related to 1.01.01)
ASTM: - - - (related to SSa-1)

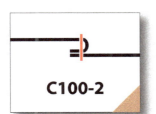

Edge Stitch / Lock Stitch

ISO: 2.02.01
ASTM: LSb-1

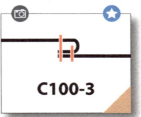

Basic Topstitch / Lock Stitch

ISO: 2.02.03
ASTM: LSq-2

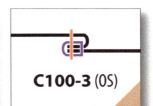

Basic Topstitch / Lock Stitch and Overlock

ISO: - - - (related to 2.02.03)
ASTM: - - - (related to LSq-2)

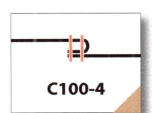

Double Topstitch / Lock Stitch

ISO: 2.02.05
ASTM: - - - (related to LSba-2)

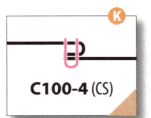

Double Topstitch / Cover Stitch

ISO: - - - (related to 2.02.05)
ASTM: - - - (related to LSb-2)

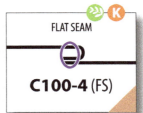

Flatlock Stitch

ISO: - - - (related to 2.02.05)
ASTM: - - - (related to LSb-2)

ABC Seams®

C100
FELLED SEAM

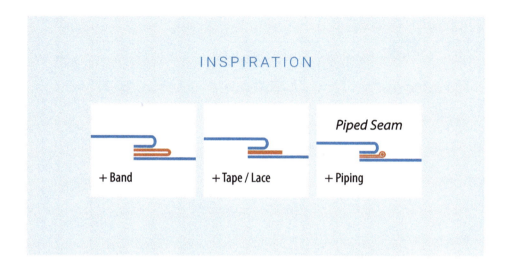

INSPIRATION

+ Band

+ Tape / Lace

Piped Seam
+ Piping

MY NOTES

101 Sewing Seams

CONSTRUCTIONS

C000
C100
C010
C101
C110
C120
C200
CD190

MY SAMPLES

Page | 33

FRENCH SEAM

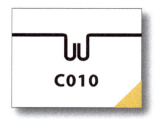

MAIN PROPERTIES

- Resistance: very good.
- Versatility: good.
- Flexibility: poor.
- Elasticity: poor.
- Cost: medium.
- Others:
Neat finishing on the inside.

COMMON USES

- High-end garments.
- Light to medium weight fabrics.
- Fabrics made of delicate materials such as silk and wool
- Sheer fabrics.
- Side seams of shirts and tops.

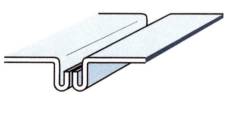

C010
FRENCH SEAM

C010-1

Without Topstitch / Lock Stitch

ISO: - - - (related to 1.06.02)
ASTM: - - - (related to SSe-2)

STEP-BY-STEP

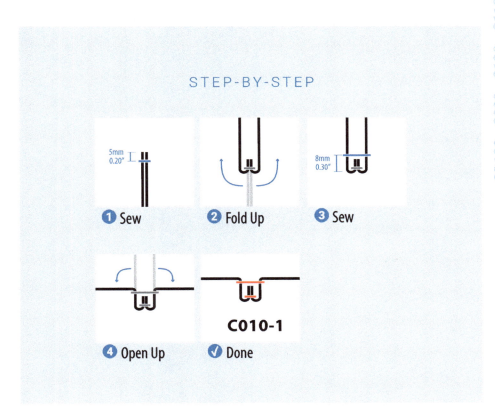

1 Sew — 5mm / 0.20"
2 Fold Up
3 Sew — 8mm / 0.30"
4 Open Up
✓ Done — C010-1

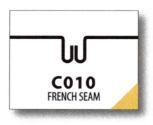

MY NOTES

MY SAMPLES

BOUND SEAM (1)

MAIN PROPERTIES

- Resistance: very good to excellent.

- Versatility: good.
It works better on medium-weight fabrics.

- Flexibility: poor to regular.

- Elasticity: poor.

- Stretch resistance.

- Cost: medium to high.

- Others:
Neat finish on the inside.
Reversible.

COMMON USES

- Give more strength to a seam.

- Decorative touch if using a contrasting or coordinating color.

- High quality garments.

- Unlined jackets, coats and outwear in general.

- Reversible garments.

- Neckline seam of T-shirts and polos (also see CD101 and CE101).

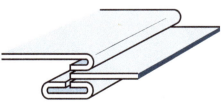

ABC Seams®

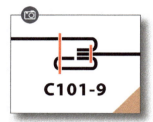
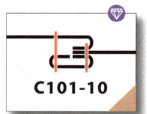
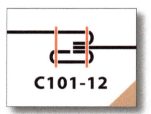

Basic Topstitch / Lock Stitch

ISO: - - - (related to 2.28.02)
ASTM: - - - (related to LSbn-2)

Basic Topstitch + Under Stitch / Lock Stitch

ISO: - - -
ASTM: - - -

Double Topstitch / Lock Stitch

ISO: 2.28.03
ASTM: - - - (related to LSl-2)

INSPIRATION

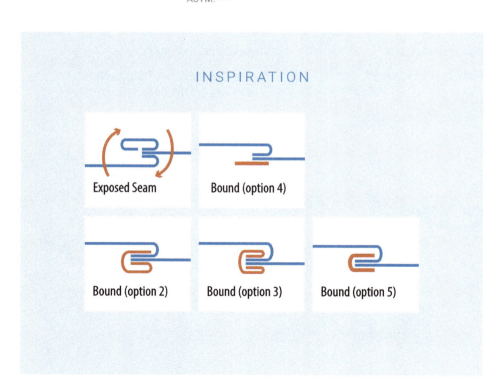

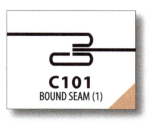

C101
BOUND SEAM (1)

MY NOTES

MY SAMPLES

WELT SEAM

C110

MAIN PROPERTIES

- Resistance: excellent.
It is one of the strongest seams.

- Versatility: very good.
It works better on straight seams or slightly curved seams.

- Flexibility: regular to good.

- Elasticity: poor.
It works as a stabilizer.

- Cost: regular.

- Others:
Also called "Flat Felled Seam", "Self Bound Seam" o "English Seam".
Neat finish on the inside.
In the industry, it's made by one step.

COMMON USES

- Shoulder and yoke seams.

- Trousers: crotch and side seams.

- Reversible garments.

- Denim garments, such as jeans, shirts, and jackets.

- Sportswear.

- Men's wear, especially shirts and work garments.

- Heavy-duty garments.

- Unlined jackets and coats.

C110-1

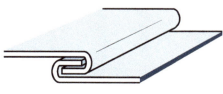

101 Sewing Seams

C110
WELT SEAM

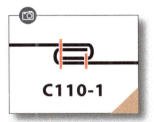

C110-1

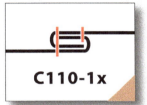

C110-1x

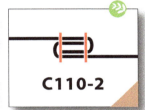

C110-2

Basic Topstitch / Lock Stitch
ISO: 2.04.06
ASTM: SSw-2

Double Topstitch / Lock Stitch
ISO: 2.04.05
ASTM: - - - (related to SSw-2)

Double Topstitch (full) / Lock Stitch
ISO: 2.04.04
ASTM: - - - (related to LSas-2)

STEP-BY-STEP

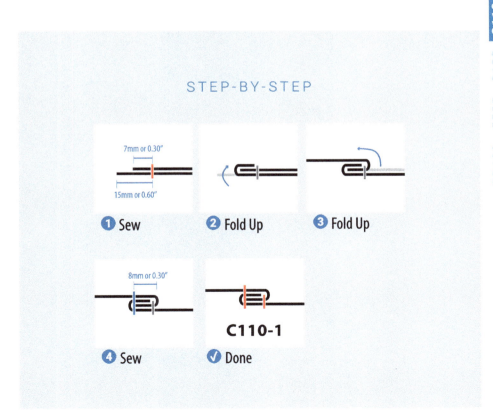

1. Sew (7mm or 0.30"; 15mm or 0.60")
2. Fold Up
3. Fold Up
4. Sew (8mm or 0.30")
✓ Done — C110-1

ABC Seams®

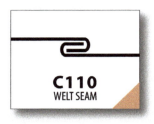

C110 WELT SEAM

MY NOTES

MY SAMPLES

LAPPED SEAM

C120

MAIN PROPERTIES

- Resistance: regular to good.

- Versatility: very good.
It is suitable for any fabric (woven and knit) and either on straight or curved seams.

- Flexibility: excellent.

- Elasticity: very good.

- Cost: low.
It is easy and quick to be made.

- Others:
Also called "Flat Seam", "Overlap Seam", "Appliqué Seam" and "Superimposed Seam".

COMMON USES

- Usually used on fabrics/materials that do not fray such as leather, PU, suede, vinyl, and laces.

- Irregular-shaped and curved seams.

- Raw and bias cut edges.

- When joining interlining, interfacing, and elastic band ends.

- Lingerie.

- Bags, footwear, and other accessories.

- Upholstery.

C120-4

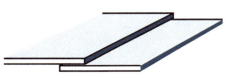

ABC Seams®

C120
LAPPED SEAM

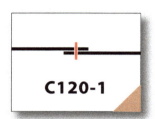   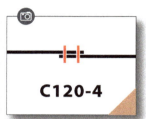   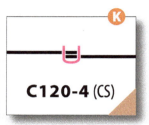

Basic Topstitch / Lock Stitch

ISO: 2.01.02
ASTM: LSa-1

Double Topstitch / Lock Stitch

ISO: - - -
ASTM: LSa-2

Double Topstitch / Cover Stitch

ISO: - - -
ASTM: - - - (related to LSa-2)

INSPIRATION

+ Band

+ Tape / Lace

+ Piping

Bounded (1)

Bounded (2)

MY NOTES

MY SAMPLES

OPEN SEAM

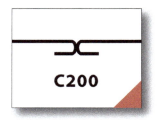

MAIN PROPERTIES

- Resistance: regular to poor.
It gets stronger when using a short stitch length to join the fabrics.

- Versatility: very good.

- Flexibility: excellent.

- Elasticity: good.

- Cost: regular.

- Others:
Also known as "Butterfly Seam" or "Plain Seam".
Good option to avoid thickness when using heavy-weight fabrics.
Seam allowance might need serged edges or topstitching.

COMMON USES

- It works better on woven fabrics of medium and heavy-weight.

- Lined garments such as jackets and coats.

- Collar stand seam.

- Side seams of formal trousers and skirts (not suitable on tight fit).

- Bags and shoes.

- Fur industry.

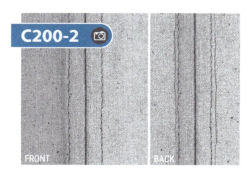

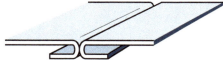

101 Sewing Seams

C200
OPEN SEAM

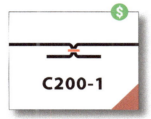

Without Topstitch / Lock Stitch

ISO: - - - (related to 1.01.01)
ASTM: - - - (related to SSa-1)

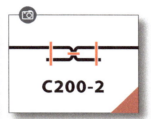

Basic Topstitch / Lock Stitch

ISO: 4.03.03
ASTM: SSz-3

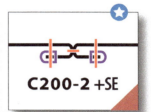

Basic Topstitch / Lock Stitch + Serged Edge

ISO: - - - (related to 4.03.03)
ASTM: - - - (related to SSz-3)

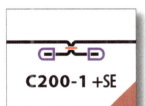

Without Topstitch / Lock Stitch + Serged Edge

ISO: 1.01.05
ASTM: - - -

Basic Topstitch / Lock Stitch / Self-Polished

ISO: - - -
ASTM: - - -

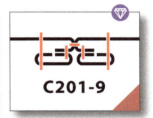

Basic Topstitch / Lock Stitch / + Bound Edge

ISO: - - -
ASTM: - - -

ABC Seams®

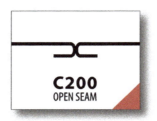

ADDITIONAL

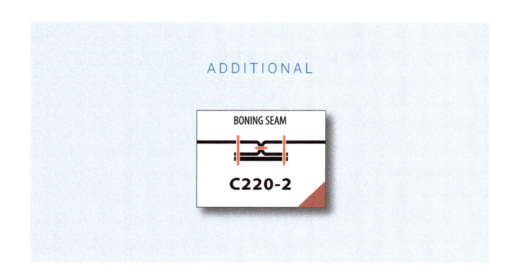

MY NOTES

101 Sewing Seams

MY SAMPLES

CONSTRUCTIONS

C000 C100 C010 C101 C110 C120 **C200** CD190

SANDWICH SEAM

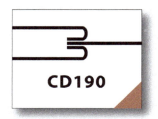

CD190

MAIN PROPERTIES

- Resistance: very good to excellent. It is stronger when adding a topstitch.

- Versatility: excellent. It is suitable for almost any fabric (woven and knit) and either on straight or curved seams.

- Flexibility: regular.

- Elasticity: poor.

- Cost: low.

- Others:
Clean finishing on both sides.
Reversible.
It prevents edge ravelling.

COMMON USES

- Lined garments.

- Necklines seam of garments with collar without collar stand.

- Yoke and shoulder seams seam of shirts and blouses.

- Cuffs.

- Waistband seam of trousers and skirts.

- Placket seam of unlined garments.

- Bags and accessories such as shoes.

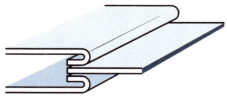

101 Sewing Seams

CONSTRUCTIONS

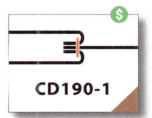

Without Topstitch /
Lock Stitch

ISO: - - -
ASTM: - - -

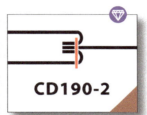

Under Stitch / Lock
Stitch

ISO: - - -
ASTM: - - - (related to LSf-2)

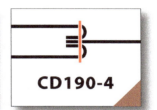

Edge Stitch / Lock
Stitch

ISO: 2.42.02
ASTM: - - - (related to LSe-2)

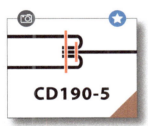

Basic Topstitch / Lock
Stitch

ISO: 2.42.04
ASTM: SSq-2

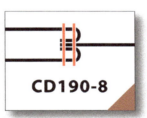

Double Topstitch /
Lock Stitch

ISO: - - -
ASTM: - - -

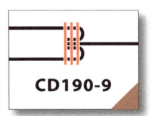

Triple Topstitch / Lock
Stitch

ISO: - - -
ASTM: - - -

Page | 51

ABC Seams®

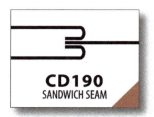

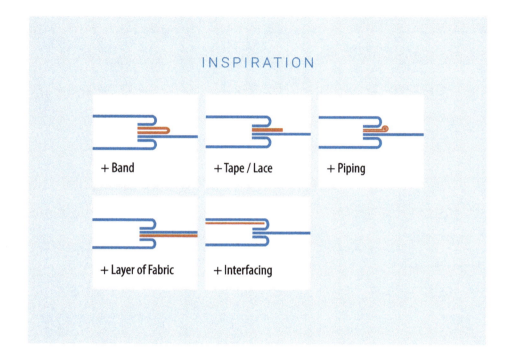

INSPIRATION

+ Band

+ Tape / Lace

+ Piping

+ Layer of Fabric

+ Interfacing

MY NOTES

101 Sewing Seams

CONSTRUCTIONS

C000 C100 C010 C101 C110 C120 C200 **CD190**

MY SAMPLES

FINISHES

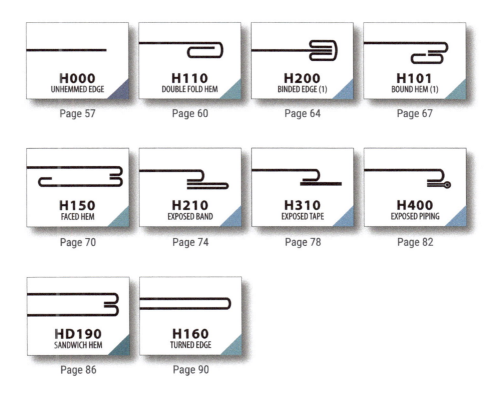

The main function of *Hems and Finishes* is to prevent the fabric edge from fraying and raveling while giving more resistance.

UNHEMMED EDGE

MAIN PROPERTIES

- Resistance: regular.
- Versatility: excellent.
- Flexibility: very good to excellent.
- Elasticity: very good to excellent.
- Cost: low.
- Others:
Also called "Flat Edge" or "Basic Edge". This group of seams includes: Raw Edge, Serged Edge, Rolled Stitch Edge. Consider if the fabrics frays or not, and what is the desired finishing.
Good option to avoid thickness when using heavy-weight fabrics.

COMMON USES

- Garments made of leather and fabrics that do not flare.
- Edges of tops and dresses made of knit fabric.
- Row-edges and unhemmed garments.
- Bottom of full skirts made in light-weight fabrics.
- Draped, curved, and bias-cut edges.
- Casual clothing / ready-to-wear garments.
- Bags and accessories.
- Upholstery.

ABC Seams®

H000
UNHEMMED EDGE

RAW EDGE

H000-0

SERGED EDGE

H000-0 +SE

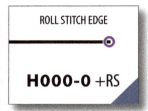

ROLL STITCH EDGE

H000-0 +RS

Without Stitch

ISO: - - -
ASTM: - - -

Overlock Stitch

ISO: - - - (related to 6.01.01)
ASTM: EFd-1

Roll Stitch

ISO: - - - (related to 6.01.01)
ASTM: - - - (related to EFd-1)

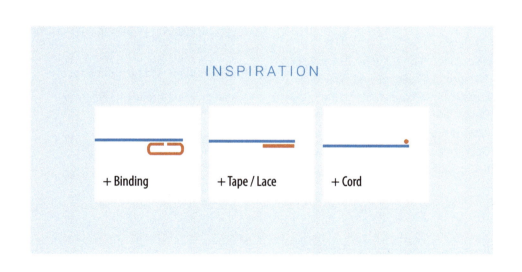

INSPIRATION

+ Binding   + Tape / Lace   + Cord

101 Sewing Seams

H000
UNHEMMED EDGE

FINISHES
H000

MY NOTES

MY SAMPLES

ABC Seams®

DOUBLE FOLD HEM

MAIN PROPERTIES

- Resistance: good to very good.

- Versatility: very good.

- Flexibility: good.

- Elasticity: good.

- Cost: low.

- Others:
Also known as "Over-welt Hem".
Hem Width: commonly made of 12mm width (1/2"). A narrow hem (H110-12) is 5 to 7 mm width (1/4"), and a Roll Hem is 3 to 5mm width (1/8").

COMMON USES

- Widely used on woven fabrics.

- Hems on woven fabrics.

- Ready-to-wear garments.

- Suitable on hems of most types of clothing and accessories: sleeves, shirts and blouses' bottoms, casual tops and dresses, skirts and trousers, children wear, bags, shoes, accessories, curtains.

- Plackets and slits.

- Pocket opening.

- Ruffles and flounces: H110-10 (Rolled Hem).

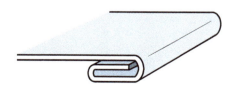

101 Sewing Seams

FINISHES

Basic Topstitch / Lock Stitch

ISO: - - - (related to 6.03.01)
ASTM: - - - (related to EFb-1)

Basic Topstitch (narrow) / Lock Stitch

ISO: - - - (related to 6.03.01)
ASTM: - - - (related to EFb-1)

Edge Stitch / Lock Stitch

ISO: - - -
ASTM: - - -

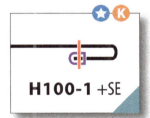

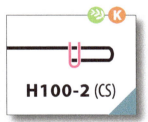

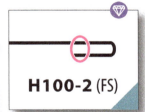

Basic Topstitch / Lock Stitch + Serged Edge

ISO: - - - (related to 6.02.01)
ASTM: - - - (related to EFa-1)

Double Topstitch / Cover Stitch

ISO: - - - (related to 6.02.03)
ASTM: - - - (related to EFa-1)

Flatlock Stitch

ISO: - - - (related to 6.02.03)
ASTM: - - - (related to EFa-1)

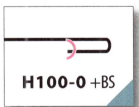

Without Topstitch / Blind Stitch

ISO: 6.02.01
ASTM: - - - (related to EFm-1)

ABC Seams®

H110
DOUBLE FOLD HEM

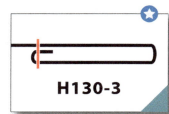

Basic Topstitch / Lock Stitch

ISO: - - -
ASTM: - - -

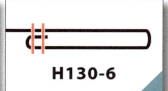

Double Basic Topstitch / Lock Stitch

ISO: - - -
ASTM: - - -

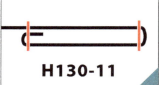

Basic Topstitch and Edge Stitch / Lock Stitch

ISO: - - - (related to 7.26.03)
ASTM: - - - (related to EFq-2)

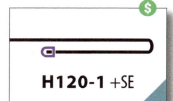

Without Topstitch / + Serged Edge

ISO: - - -
ASTM: - - -

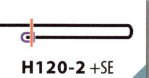

Basic Topstitch / Lock Stitch + Serged Edge

ISO: - - -
ASTM: - - -

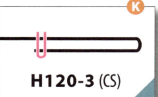

Double Topstitch / Cover Stitch

ISO: - - -
ASTM: - - -

MY NOTES

MY SAMPLES

BINDED EDGE (1)

MAIN PROPERTIES

- Resistance: excellent.

- Versatility: very good.
The binding requires the same care techniques as the main fabric.

- Flexibility: good.

- Elasticity: poor, except when using a stretchable binding.

- Cost: medium.

- Others:
Also known as "Bias Bound Edge".
Neat finish on both sides.
The binding reinforces the edge adding more structure. It also gives a decorative touch if using contrasting.

COMMON USES

- Ready-to-wear garments.

- Sportswear.

- Lingerie and swimsuits.

- Reversible garments.

- Accessories: bags, footwear, home-decor and the fury industry.

- Curved edges and edges cut on the bias.

- Necklines of T-shirts, tops, and dresses.

- Sleeve hems.

- Armhole edges of singlets or sleeveless tops/dresses.

- Slits on cuffs.

- Plackets.

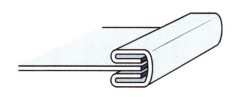

H200
BINDED EDGE (1)

 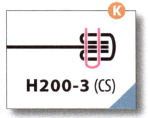

Edge Stitch / Lock Stitch

ISO: 3.05.01
ASTM: BSc-1

Double Topstitch / Cover Stitch

ISO: - - - (related to 3.05.12)
ASTM: - - - (related to BSc-2)

INSPIRATION

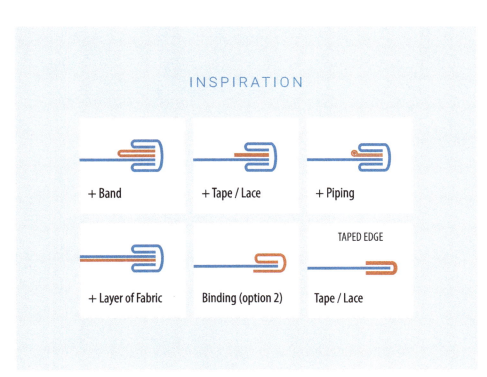

ABC Seams®

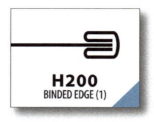

MY NOTES

MY SAMPLES

BOUND HEM (1)

MAIN PROPERTIES

- Resistance: very good.

- Versatility: very good.
It works in almost any fabric (woven and knit), either for straight or curved hems.

- Flexibility: regular.

- Elasticity: poor.
Poor elongation recovery.

- Cost: medium to high.

- Others:
Also known as "Hong Kong Finishing".
Good choice to add extra weight to the hem.
Hem-Width is usually between 7 and 10 mm wide (0.25" to 0.4").

COMMON USES

- High-quality garments.

- Curved edges and edges cut on the bias.

- Necklines.

- Armholes (sleeveless garments).

- Bottoms and cuffs.

- Narrow plackets.

- Opening edge of patch pockets.

- Reversible garments.

- Bags and accessories.

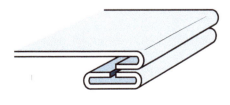

ABC Seams®

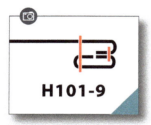
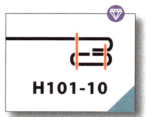
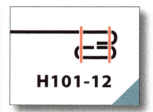

Basic Topstitch / Lock Stitch

ISO: - - - (related to 7.32.02)
ASTM: - - -

Basic Topstitch + Understitch / Lock Stitch

ISO: - - -
ASTM: - - -

Double Topstitch / Lock Stitch

ISO: 7.32.03
ASTM: LSk-2

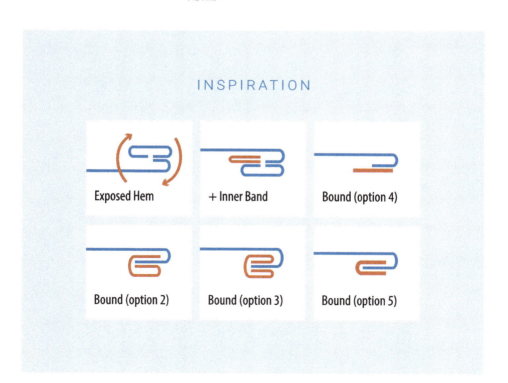

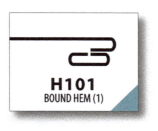

MY NOTES

MY SAMPLES

FACED HEM

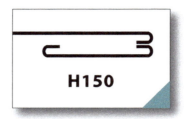

H150

MAIN PROPERTIES

- Resistance: good to very good.
It is stronger when adding interfacing.

- Versatility: good to very good.
It works perfect on woven fabrics, either on straight and curved hems.
- Flexibility: good.

- Elasticity: poor to regular.

- Cost: medium.

- Others:
Neat finishing on the inside.
It works better on wovens.
A piece of interfacing might be needed to get the best result.
The facing stabilizes the edge.

COMMON USES

- Necklines and armholes of sleeveless tops and dresses.

- Plackets of shirts, blouses, and jackets.

- Bottoms of sleeves, tops, dresses, and skirts.

- Bottoms of unlined jackets and coats.

- Curved hems and hems cut on the bias.

- Cuffs and cuff vents.

- Waistband of skirts and formal pants.

- Pocket opening.

- Reversible garments.

- Bags, shoes, and home decor.

H150-31

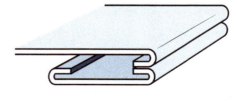

101 Sewing Seams

H150
FACED HEM

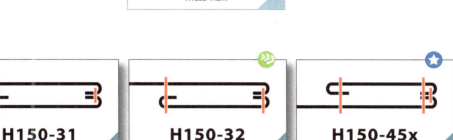

H150-31
Basic Topstitch / Lock Stitch
ISO: - - - (related to 7.32.02)
ASTM: - - - (related to LSct-2)

H150-32
Basic Topstitch and Understitch / Lock Stitch
ISO: - - -
ASTM: - - -

H150-45x
Exposed Facing with Flap and Double Topstitch / Lock Stitch
ISO: - - - (related to 7.32.01)
ASTM: - - - (related to LSk-2)

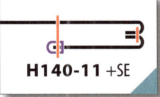

H140-11 +SE
Basic Topstitch / Lock Stitch + Serged Edge
ISO: - - -
ASTM: - - -

H140-12 +SE
Basic Topstitch and Understitch / Lock Stitch + Serged Edge
ISO: - - - (related to 7.33.01)
ASTM: - - - (related to Lsag-2)

INSPIRATION

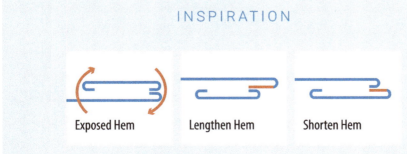

Exposed Hem   Lengthen Hem   Shorten Hem

ABC Seams®

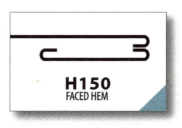

H150
FACED HEM

MY NOTES

MY SAMPLES

EXPOSED BAND

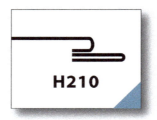

MAIN PROPERTIES

- Resistance: good.

- Versatility: excellent.
Suitable for almost any fabric, either on straight and curved edges.
When sewing curved edges, it works better if the binding is cut on the bias.

- Flexibility: good.

- Elasticity: good to poor.
The elongation recovery improves when the band is made of knit fabric or cut on the bias.

- Cost: regular.

- Others:
Also known as "Banded Hem".

COMMON USES

- Commonly used on garments made of knit fabrics such as T-shirts and sweatshirts.

- Sportswear.

- Curved edges or edges cut on the bias.

- Necklines of T-shirts, tops and dresses.

- Shirts and blouses cuffs.

- Armhole edges of singlets or sleeveless tops/dresses.

- Waistbands with elastic band.

- Gathered hems with elastic band.

- Knitted cuffs and bottoms (wide band, usually made of rib), for instance, joggings.

H210-1 (OS)

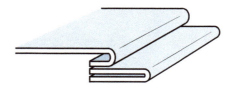

101 Sewing Seams

FINISHES

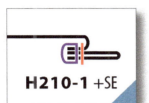

Without Topstitch / Lock Stitch + Serged Edge

ISO: - - -
ASTM: - - -

Without Topstitch / Overlock Stitch

ISO: - - -
ASTM: - - -

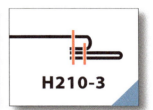

Basic Topstitch / Lock Stitch

ISO: - - -
ASTM: - - -

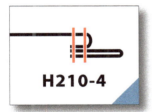

Double Topstitch / Lock Stitch

ISO: - - -
ASTM: - - -

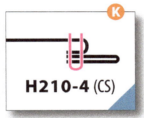

Double Topstitch / Cover Stitch

ISO: - - -
ASTM: - - -

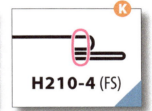

Flatlock Stitch

ISO: - - -
ASTM: - - -

ADDITIONAL

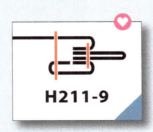

Page | 75

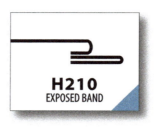

MY NOTES

MY SAMPLES

EXPOSED TAPE

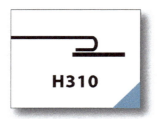

MAIN PROPERTIES

- Resistance: good to very good.

- Versatility: very good.
Suitable for almost any fabric.
It works better on straight seams.
The tape (or lace) requires the same care techniques as the main fabric.

- Flexibility: good.

- Elasticity: good to poor.

- Cost: regular.

- Others:
Also known as "Taped Hem".
The tape (or lace) adds a decorative touch if using contrasting or coordinating color.

COMMON USES

- Sportswear.

- Lingerie and swimsuits.

- Shirts and blouses cuffs.

- Ribbed necklines and cuffs of polo shirts.

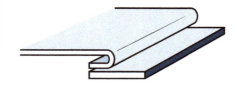

101 Sewing Seams

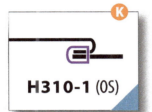

Without Topstitch / Overlock Stitch

ISO: - - -
ASTM: - - -

Basic Topstitch / Lock Stitch

ISO: - - -
ASTM: - - -

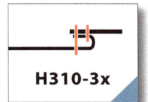

Exposed Tape with Double Topstitch / Lock Stitch

ISO: - - -
ASTM: - - -

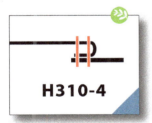

Double Topstitch / Lock Stitch

ISO: - - -
ASTM: - - -

ADDITIONAL

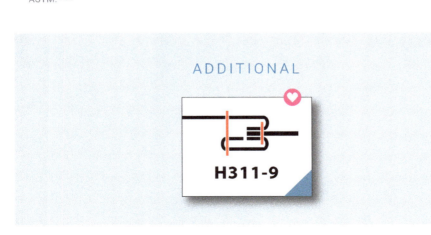

Page | 79

ABC Seams®

MY NOTES

MY SAMPLES

EXPOSED PIPING

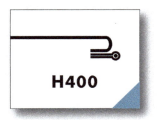

MAIN PROPERTIES

- Resistance: good to very good.

- Versatility: good.
Suitable for almost any fabric, either on straight and curved edges.
The piping requires the same care techniques as the main fabric.

- Flexibility: good.

- Elasticity: good to poor.

- Cost: regular.

- Others:
Also known as "Piped Hem".
The corded piping adds more structure to the hem.

COMMON USES

- Ready-to-wear garments.

- Sportswear.

- Lingerie and swimsuits.

- Sleeve hems.

- Accessories.

- Fur industry.

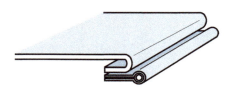

101 Sewing Seams

H400
EXPOSED PIPING

H400-1

Without Topstitch / Lock Stitch

ISO: - - -
ASTM: - - -

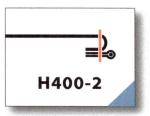

H400-2

Edge Stitch / Lock Stitch

ISO: - - -
ASTM: - - -

H400-3

Basic Topstitch / Lock Stitch

ISO: - - -
ASTM: - - -

H400-4

Double Topstitch / Lock Stitch

ISO: - - -
ASTM: - - -

ADDITIONAL

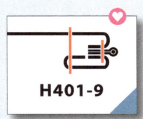

H401-9

Page | 83

ABC Seams®

MY NOTES

MY SAMPLES

SANDWICH HEM

HD190

MAIN PROPERTIES

- Resistance: good to very good.
- Versatility: excellent.
Suitable for almost any fabric (woven and knit), either for straight or curved hems.
- Flexibility: good.
- Elasticity: regular to poor.
- Cost: low.
- Others:
Interfacing (or interlining) is optional.
Neat finishing on the inside.
Reversible: the wrong side can be used as the right side.

COMMON USES

- Lined garments: bottoms, necklines, cuffs, and sleeves.
- Reversible garments.
- Collars and hoods.
- Curved and cut on the bias edges.
- Lapel edges.
- Edges of pocket depths.
- Keyhole cut-out.
- Bags, shoes, and accessories.

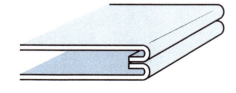

101 Sewing Seams

Without Topstitch / Lock Stitch

ISO: - - - (related to 1.01.01)
ASTM: - - - (related to Ssa-1)

Understitch / Lock Stitch

ISO: - - -
ASTM: - - -

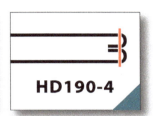

Edge Stitch / Lock Stitch

ISO: 1.06.01
ASTM: SSc-1

Basic Topstitch / Lock Stitch

ISO: 1.06.02
ASTM: Sse-2

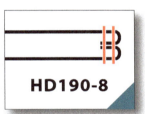

Double Topstitch / Lock Stitch

ISO: 1.06.04
ASTM: - - -

Double Topstitch Off-Seam / Lock Stitch

ISO: - - -
ASTM: - - -

Page | 87

ABC Seams®

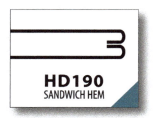

HD190
SANDWICH HEM

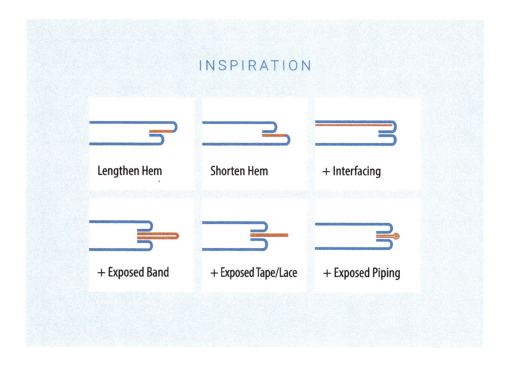

INSPIRATION

Lengthen Hem | Shorten Hem | + Interfacing
+ Exposed Band | + Exposed Tape/Lace | + Exposed Piping

MY NOTES

101 Sewing Seams

MY SAMPLES

FINISHES

H000 H110 H200 H101 H150 H210 H310 H400 **HD190** H160

TURNED EDGE

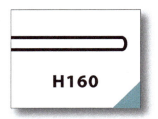

H160

MAIN PROPERTIES

- Resistance: very good.

- Versatility: excellent.
It suits to a wide variety of fabrics.

- Flexibility: excellent.

- Elasticity: very good to excellent.

- Cost: low.

- Others:
Also known as "folded edge" and "turned hem".
Using interfacing might be needed to get the best results.
Good option to avoid thickness when using heavy-weight fabrics.

COMMON USES

- Lined and reversible garments.

- Bottoms and bottom sleeves of jacket sleeves.

- Shirt cuff edges.

- Bib, cow collars, and turtlenecks.

- Accessories: bags, footwear, home-decor.

- Upholstery.

H160-0

FRONT

BACK

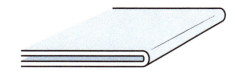

101 Sewing Seams

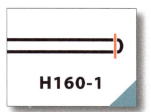

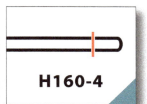

Without Topstitch
ISO: - - -
ASTM: - - -

Edge Stitch / Lock Stitch
ISO: - - - (related to 5.45.01)
ASTM: OSf-1

Basic Topstitch / Lock Stitch
ISO: 5.45.01
ASTM: - - - (related to OSf-1)

INSPIRATION

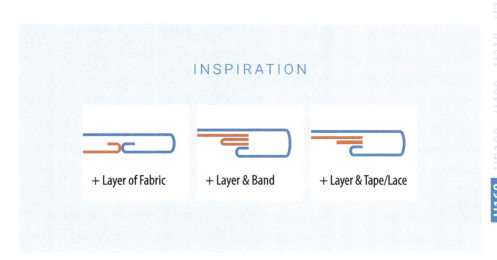

+ Layer of Fabric   + Layer & Band   + Layer & Tape/Lace

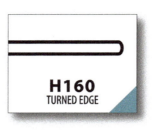

MY NOTES

MY SAMPLES

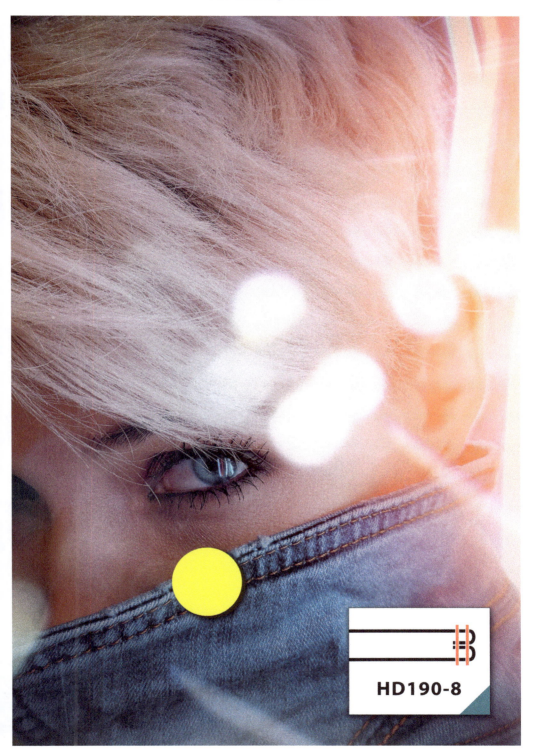

DETAILS

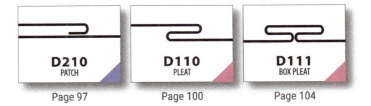

The *Details* category includes those seams that embellish the design, give volume, and join pieces on the fabric.

PATCH

MAIN PROPERTIES

- Resistance: very good to excellent.
- Versatility: very good.
- Flexibility: good.
- Elasticity: poor.
- Cost: medium.
- Others:
Reversible.
Clean finish on both sides.

COMMON USES

- Work clothing.
- Side seam of Patch Pockets (including Kangaroo Pocket).
- Upper edge of Flap Pockets.
- Pants: facing edge of side pockets.
- Elbow patches.
- Inner back yoke of polo-shirts.
- Bags, shoes, and accessories.
- Appliqué for fabrics that fray easily.

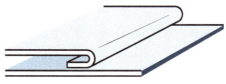

ABC Seams®

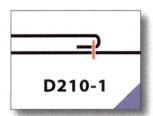
Without Topstitch /
Lock Stitch

ISO: - - - (related to 1.02.01)
ASTM: - - - (related to SSbd-1)

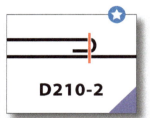
Edge Stitch / Lock Stitch

ISO: 5.31.02
ASTM: LSd-1

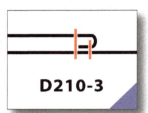
Basic Topstitch / Lock Stitch

ISO: 5.31.04
ASTM: LSbk-2

Double Topstitch /
Lock Stitch

ISO: - - - (related to 5.31.03)
ASTM: LSd-2

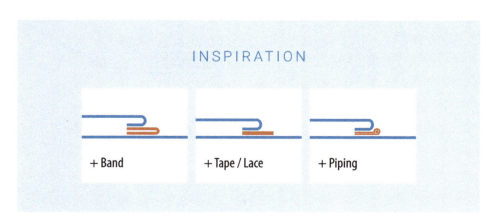

INSPIRATION

+ Band   + Tape / Lace   + Piping

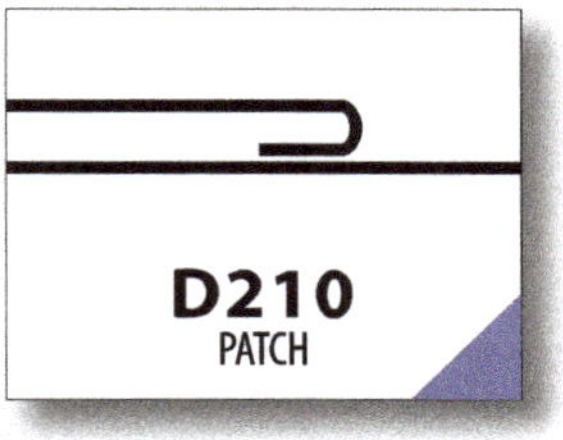

101 Sewing Seams

D210
PATCH

DETAILS
D210
D110
D111

MY NOTES

MY SAMPLES

Page | 99

PLEAT

D110

MAIN PROPERTIES

- Resistance: regular to good.
It is stronger when it's closed or when adding a topstitch.

- Versatility: excellent.
It is suitable for any fabric (woven and knit).

- Flexibility: good to very good.

- Elasticity: good.

- Cost: low to medium.

- Others:
When it's open, it gives volume to the fabric. And when it's closed, it reduces the volume.
This group includes: darts and tucks.

COMMON USES

- Mostly used on wovens to give or reduce volumes.

- Commonly used on waist, hip, and bust areas of women's clothing.

- Skirts and pants.

- Children wear.

- Cuff seam of shirts and blouses.

- Back yoke of shirts and blouses.

- Inner back of lined outerwear.

- Patch pockets.

- Bags and shoes.

- Accessories such as hats.

- Home décor items (curtains, pillowcases).

- Upholstery.

D110-0

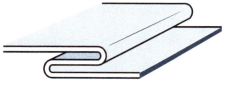

101 Sewing Seams

 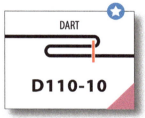 

Without Topstitch

ISO: - - -
ASTM: - - -

Without Topstitch / Lock Stitch

ISO: - - - (related to 5.45.01)
ASTM: - - - (related to OSf-1)

Basic Topstitch / Lock Stitch

ISO: - - -
ASTM: - - -

ADDITIONAL

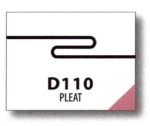

MY NOTES

MY SAMPLES

BOX PLEAT

MAIN PROPERTIES

- Resistance: good to very good.
It is stronger when it's closed or when adding a topstitch.

- Versatility: very good.
It is suitable for almost any fabric. It could be too thick and stiff when using heavy-weight fabrics.

- Flexibility: regular.

- Elasticity: regular to poor.

- Cost: low to medium.

- Others:
Reversible: when using the back-side facing up, it's called "Inverted Box Pleat" (group D112), and it looks flat and clean.

COMMON USES

- Skirts and pants.
- Children wear.
- Back yoke of shirts and blouses.
- Inner back of lined outerwear.
- Patch pockets.
- Bags and accessories.

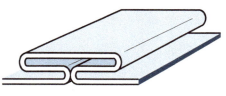

D111 BOX PLEAT

D111-0

Without Topstitch

ISO: - - -
ASTM: - - -

D111-0A

Without Topstitch / Lock Stitch

ISO: - - - (related to 5.45.01)
ASTM: - - - (related to OSf-1)

D111-1

Edge Stitch / Lock Stitch

ISO: - - -
ASTM: - - -

D112-0A

Without Topstitch / Lock Stitch

ISO: - - - (related to 5.45.01)
ASTM: - - - (related to OSf-1)

D112-1

Without Topstitch with Inner Edge Stitch / Lock Stitch

ISO: - - -
ASTM: - - -

D112-5

Edge Stitch / Lock Stitch

ISO: - - -
ASTM: - - -

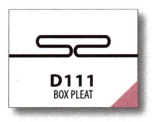

MY NOTES

MY SAMPLES

OVERVIEW

ABC Seams®

101 SEWING SEAMS

CONSTRUCTION — P. 27

C000 BASIC SEAM	C000-1	C000-1 (OS)
C100-3 (OS)	C100-4	C100-4 (CS)
C100-4 (FS)	**C010** FRENCH SEAM — P. 34	
C110-1x	C110-2	**C120** LAPPED SEAM — P. 43
C120-1	C120-4	
C201-9	C220-2	**CD190** SANDWICH SEAM — P. 50
CD190-1	CD190-2	
H000-0 +SE	H000-0 +RS	**H110** DOUBLE FOLD HEM — P. 60
H110-2	H110-12	
H130-11	H120-1 +SE	H120-2 +SE
H120-3 (CS)	**H200** BINDED EDGE (1) — P. 64	
H150-31	H150-32	H150-45x
H140-11 +SE	H140-12 +SE	
H211-9	**H310** EXPOSED TAPE — P. 78	H310-1 (OS)
H310-3	H310-3x	
H401-9	**HD190** SANDWICH HEM — P. 86	HD190-1
HD190-2	HD190-4	

DETAILS — P. 97

	D210 PATCH / SELF POLISHED	D210-1
D210-2	D210-3	
D111-0	D111-0A	D111-1
D112-0A	D112-1	

Page | 108

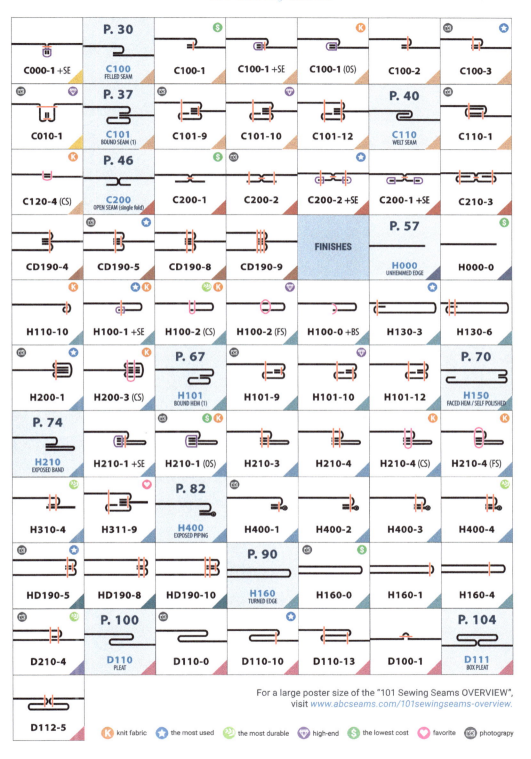

Part Three

REFERENCE MATERIAL

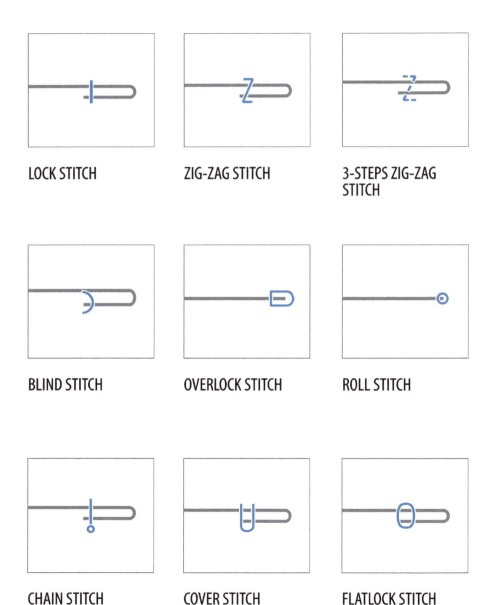

MY SAMPLES

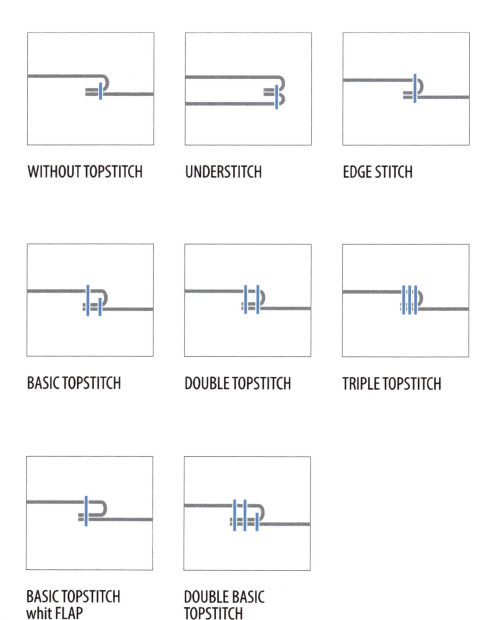

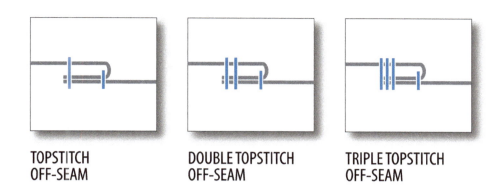

TOPSTITCH OFF-SEAM

DOUBLE TOPSTITCH OFF-SEAM

TRIPLE TOPSTITCH OFF-SEAM

MY SAMPLES

TECHNICAL SPECIFICATIONS

Page 126

Page 132

Page 128

Page 140

ABC Seams®

STYLE:	**MARC**
Code:	#04-968
Fabric:	Cotton 7458 / 185 g. / color 238
Description:	Classic t-shirt slim fit

SEAMS REFERENCE

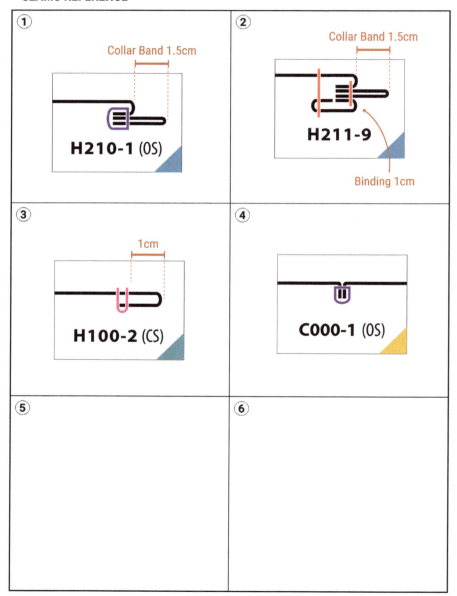

101 Sewing Seams

Season: **SS22**	Designer: **Arnau**
Collection: **Basics**	Supplier: **PITU Tex**
Range Size: **XS, S, M, L, XL**	Delivery Date: **20/02/21**
Proto Size: **M** PROTOTYPE	Due Date: **02/03/21**

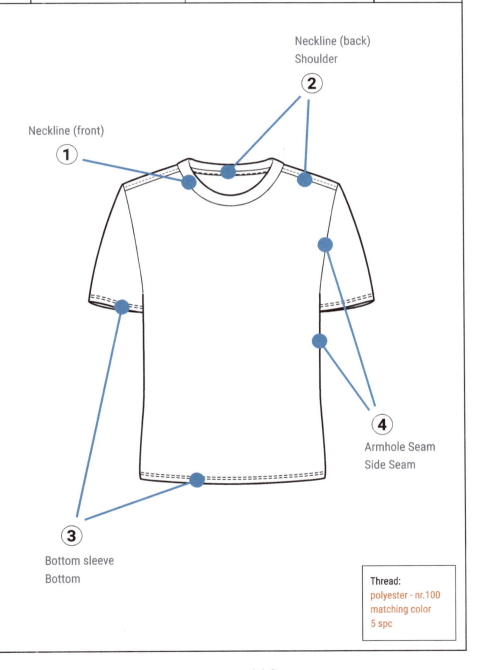

Neckline (front)
①

Neckline (back)
Shoulder
②

Bottom sleeve
Bottom
③

Armhole Seam
Side Seam
④

Thread:
polyester - nr.100
matching color
5 spc

STYLE:	**FRANCIS**
Code:	#06-719
Fabric:	Pique 08349 / 200 g. / color 825
Description:	Polo shirt with rib

SEAMS REFERENCE

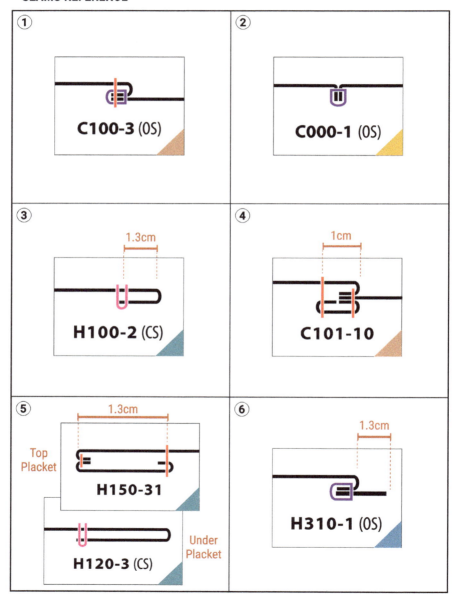

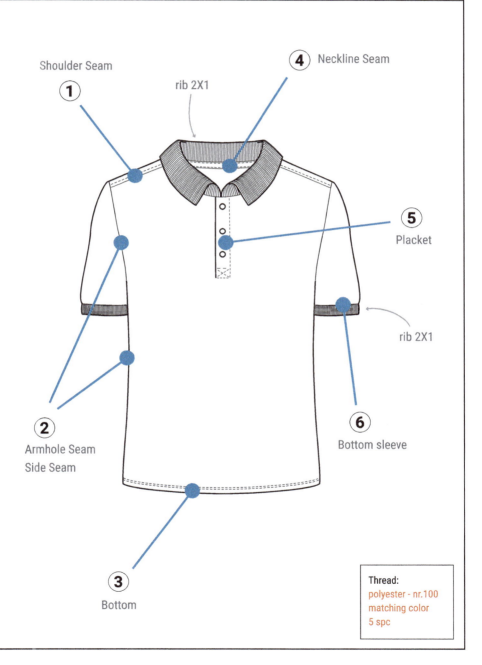

STYLE:	**LOUIS**
Code:	#07-342
Fabric:	Cotton 2436 / 170 g. / color 008
Description:	Classic shirt with chest pocket

SEAMS REFERENCE

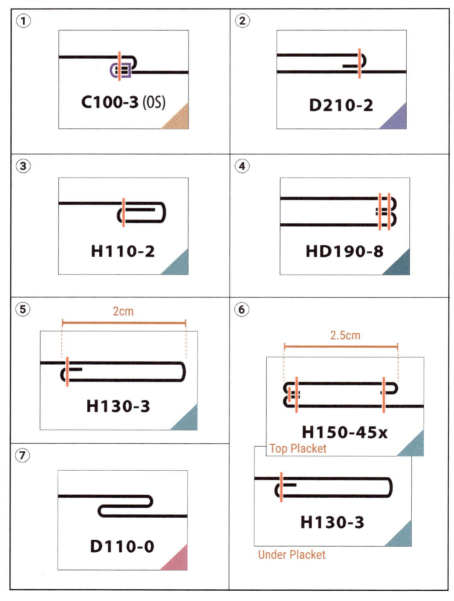

101 Sewing Seams

Season:	SS22	Designer:	Aleks
Collection:	Basics	Supplier:	PITU Tex
Range Size:	XS, S, M, L, XL	Delivery Date:	20/02/21
Proto Size:	M PROTOTYPE	Due Date:	02/03/21

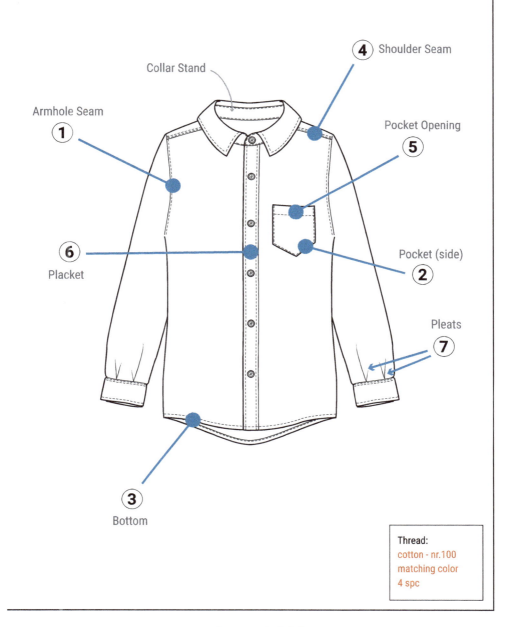

Thread:
cotton - nr.100
matching color
4 spc

Page | 123

ABC Seams®

STYLE: **LOUIS**
Code: #07-342
Fabric: Cotton 2436 / 170 g. / color 008
Description: Classic shirt with chest pocket

SEAMS REFERENCE

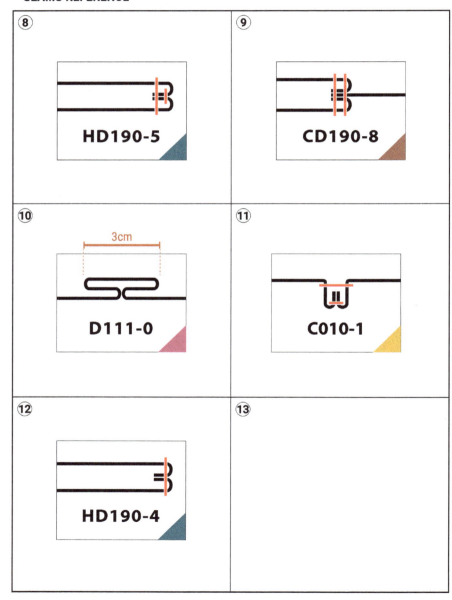

101 Sewing Seams

Season:	SS22	Designer:	Aleks
Collection:	Basics	Supplier:	PITU Tex
Range Size:	XS, S, M, L, XL	Delivery Date:	20/02/21
Proto Size:	M PROTOTYPE	Due Date:	02/03/21

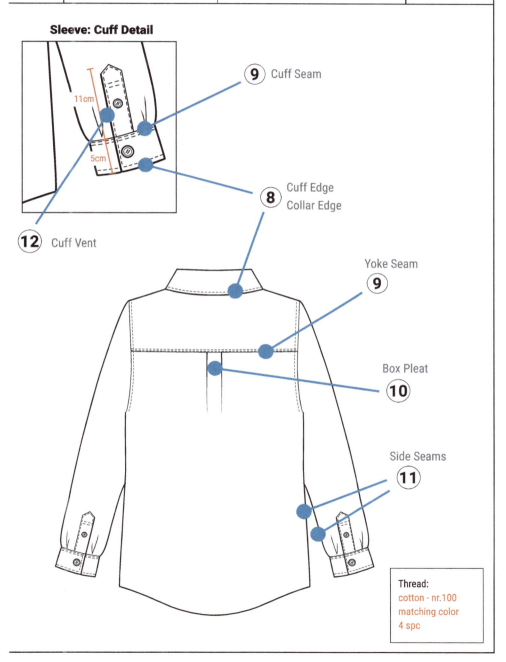

Sleeve: Cuff Detail

11cm

5cm

(9) Cuff Seam

(8) Cuff Edge / Collar Edge

(12) Cuff Vent

Yoke Seam (9)

Box Pleat (10)

Side Seams (11)

Thread:
cotton - nr.100
matching color
4 spc

ABC Seams®

STYLE:	**PACHA**
Code:	**#02-343**
Fabric:	**Silk 0254 / 150 g. / color 008**
Description:	**Boat neckline blouse**

SEAMS REFERENCE

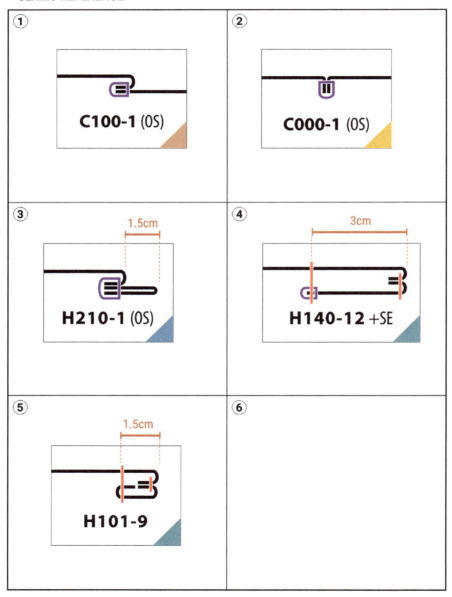

① C100-1 (OS)
② C000-1 (OS)
③ H210-1 (OS) — 1.5cm
④ H140-12 +SE — 3cm
⑤ H101-9 — 1.5cm
⑥

101 Sewing Seams

Season:	SS22	Designer:	Tory
Collection:	Basics	Supplier:	PITU Tex
Range Size:	XS, S, M, L, XL	Delivery Date:	20/02/21
Proto Size:	S PROTOTYPE	Due Date:	02/03/21

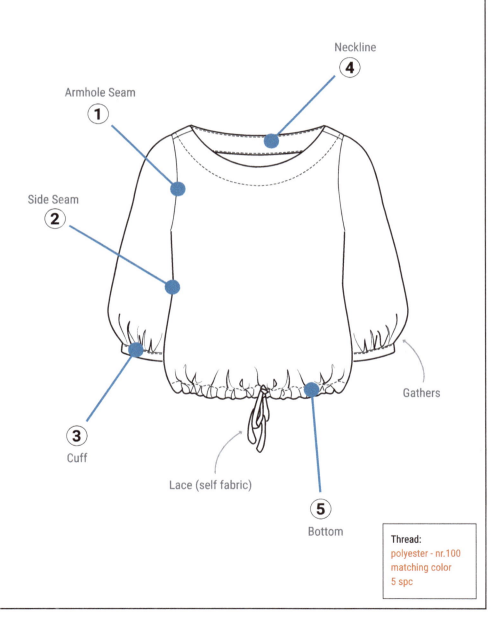

- ① Armhole Seam
- ② Side Seam
- ③ Cuff
- ④ Neckline
- ⑤ Bottom
- Gathers
- Lace (self fabric)

Thread:
polyester - nr.100
matching color
5 spc

ABC Seams®

STYLE:	**HAUTS**
Code:	**#04-968**
Fabric:	**Denim 0256 / 11 oz / color 252**
Description:	**5 pocket jeans**

SEAMS REFERENCE

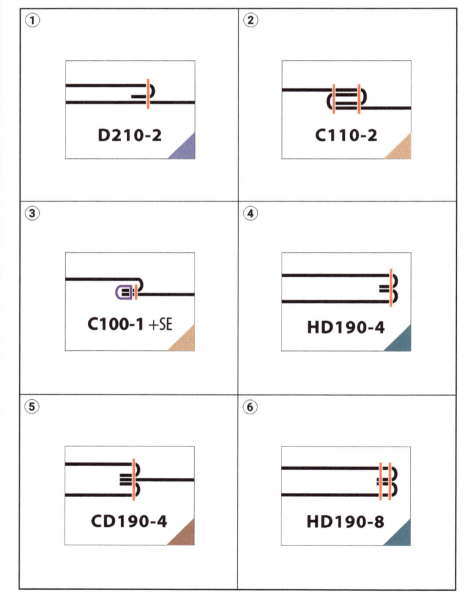

Page | 128

101 Sewing Seams

Season: **SS22**	Designer: **Jessica**
Collection: **Basics**	Supplier: **PITU Tex**
Range Size: **36, 38, 40, 42, 44**	Delivery Date: **20/02/21**
Proto Size: **40** **PROTOTYPE**	Due Date: **02/03/21**

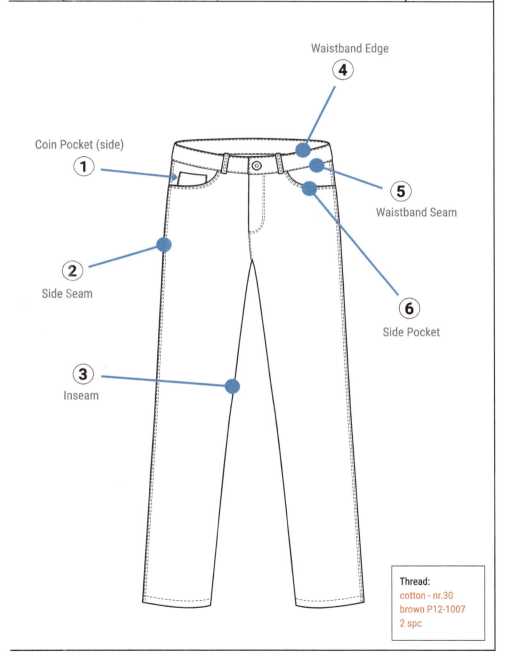

- 1 — Coin Pocket (side)
- 2 — Side Seam
- 3 — Inseam
- 4 — Waistband Edge
- 5 — Waistband Seam
- 6 — Side Pocket

Thread:
cotton - nr.30
brown P12-1007
2 spc

STYLE:	**HAUTS**
Code:	**#04-968**
Fabric:	**Denim 0256 / 11 oz / color 252**
Description:	**5 pocket jeans**

SEAMS REFERENCE

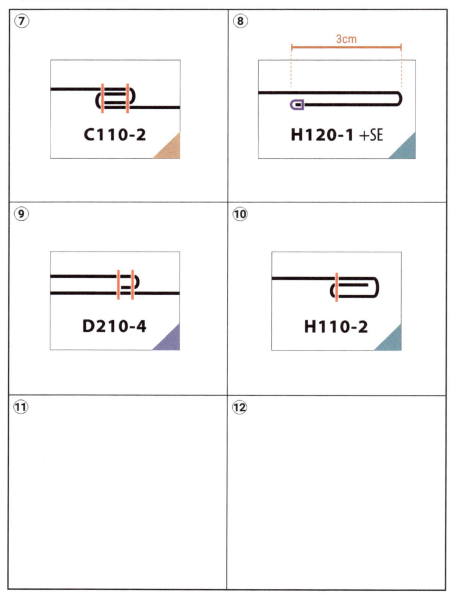

101 Sewing Seams

Season:	SS22	Designer:	Jessica
Collection:	Basics	Supplier:	PITU Tex
Range Size:	36, 38, 40, 42, 44	Delivery Date:	20/02/21
Proto Size:	40 PROTOTYPE	Due Date:	02/03/21

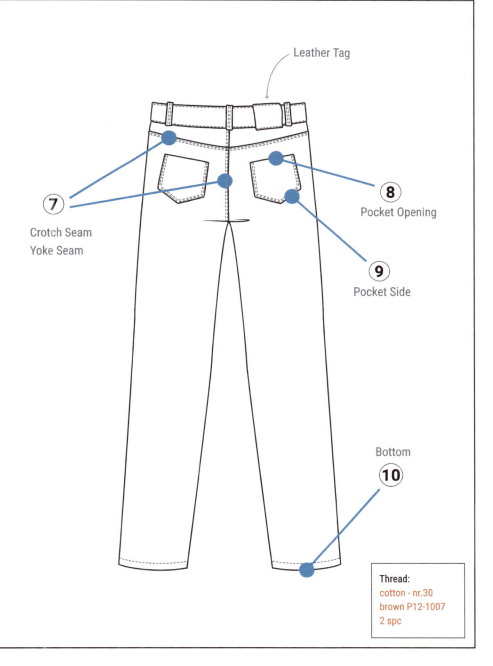

Leather Tag

7 Crotch Seam
Yoke Seam

8 Pocket Opening

9 Pocket Side

Bottom
10

Thread:
cotton - nr.30
brown P12-1007
2 spc

ABC Seams®

STYLE: **NINALU**
Code: **#04-968**
Fabric: **Cotton 3256 / 250 g. / color 008**
Description: **Classic trench with end-plate**

SEAMS REFERENCE

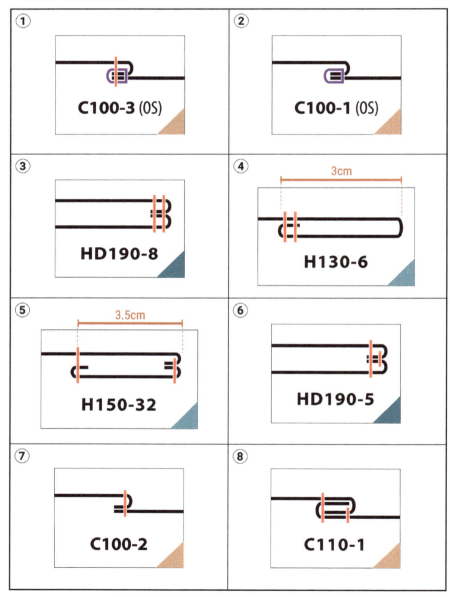

101 Sewing Seams

Season:	SS22	Designer:	Marina
Collection:	Basics	Supplier:	PITU Tex
Range Size:	XS, S, M, L, XL	Delivery Date:	20/02/21
Proto Size:	S PROTOTYPE	Due Date:	02/03/21

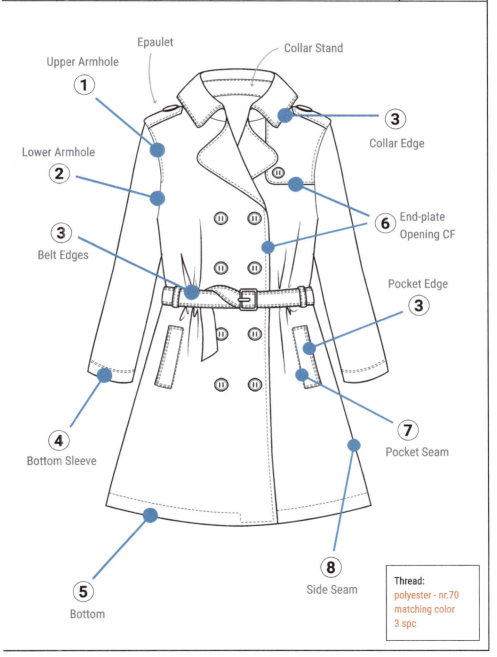

- Epaulet
- Collar Stand
- Upper Armhole — ①
- ③ Collar Edge
- Lower Armhole — ②
- ⑥ End-plate Opening CF
- ③ Belt Edges
- Pocket Edge ③
- ⑦ Pocket Seam
- ④ Bottom Sleeve
- ⑧ Side Seam
- ⑤ Bottom

Thread:
polyester - nr.70
matching color
3 spc

STYLE: **CHILLI**

Code: **#11-324**

Fabric: **Cotton 6374 / 200 g. / color 825**

Description: **Paneled pleated skirt**

SEAMS REFERENCE

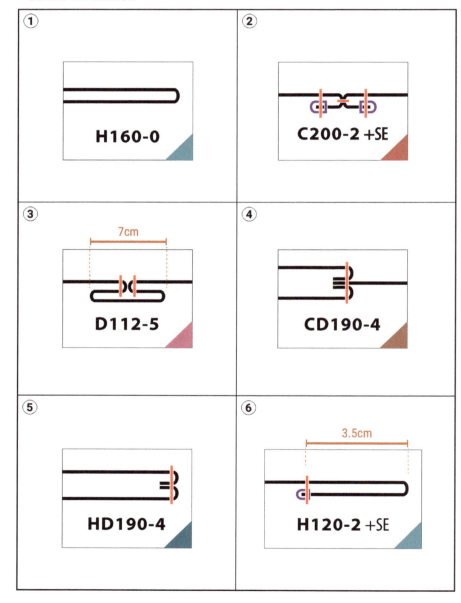

101 Sewing Seams

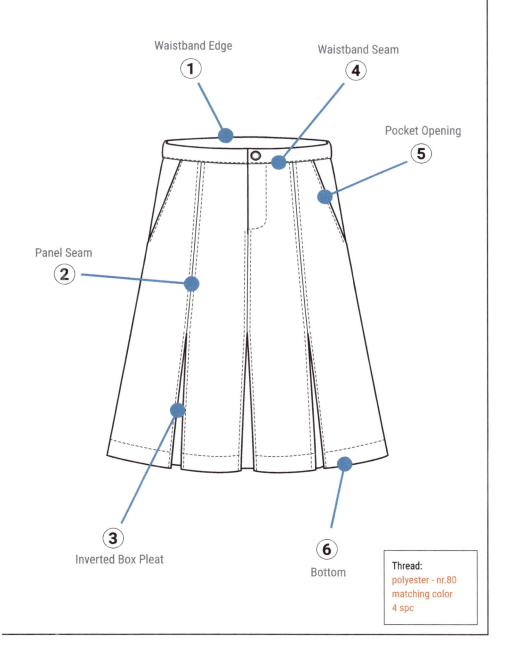

ABC Seams®

STYLE: **FABIEN**
Code: **#04-968**
Fabric: **Lycra 0036 / 170 g. / color 252**
Description: **String bikini**

SEAMS REFERENCE

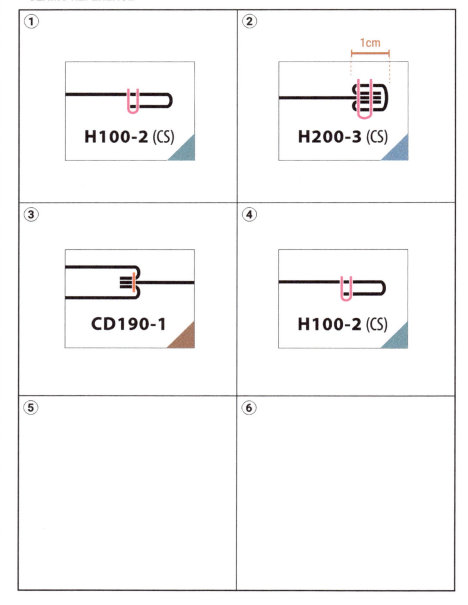

101 Sewing Seams

Season:	**SS22**	Designer:	**Mary**
Collection:	**Basics**	Supplier:	**PITU Tex**
Range Size:	**XS, S, M, L, XL**	Delivery Date:	**20/02/21**
Proto Size:	**S** PROTOTYPE	Due Date:	**02/03/21**

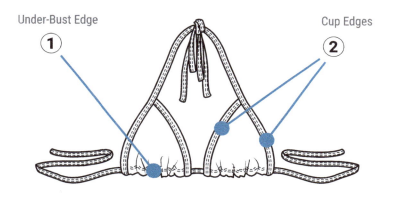

Under-Bust Edge — 1
Cup Edges — 2

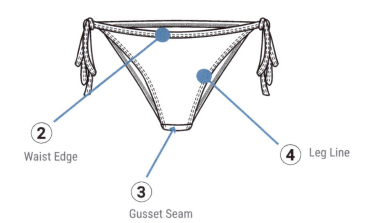

Waist Edge — 2
Gusset Seam — 3
Leg Line — 4

Thread:
wooly-poly
matching color
6 spc

Page | 137

ABC Seams®

STYLE: **LINA**
Code: **#04-968**
Fabric: **Cotton 7398 / 160 g. / color 238**
Description: **Short sleeve dress with pintucks**

SEAMS REFERENCE

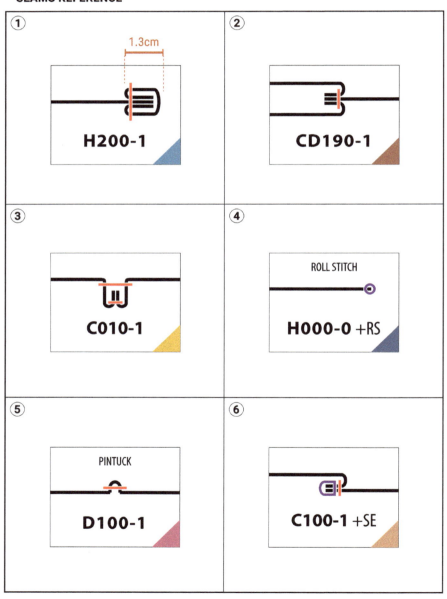

101 Sewing Seams

Season:	SS22	Designer:	Annie
Collection:	Basics	Supplier:	PITU Tex
Range Size:	2, 3, 4, 5, 6	Delivery Date:	20/02/21
Proto Size:	4 PROTOTYPE	Due Date:	02/03/21

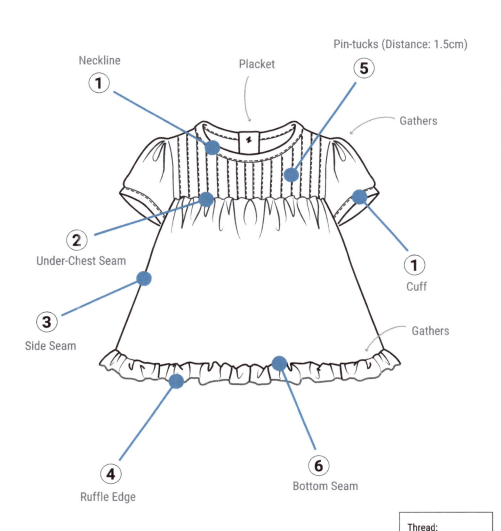

Neckline — 1
Placket
Pin-tucks (Distance: 1.5cm) — 5
Gathers
Under-Chest Seam — 2
Cuff — 1
Side Seam — 3
Gathers
Ruffle Edge — 4
Bottom Seam — 6

Thread:
polyester - nr.100
pink P19-5687
6 spc

ABC Seams®

STYLE:	**LOLA**
Code:	**#04-968**
Fabric:	**PVU 3254 / 280 g. / color 008**
Description:	**Panelled tote bag**

SEAMS REFERENCE

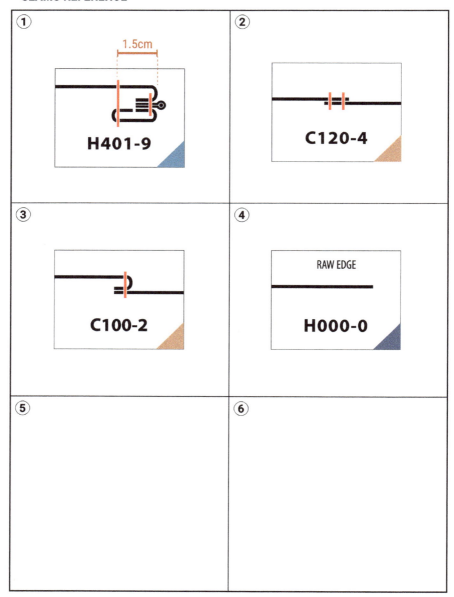

① H401-9 — 1.5cm
② C120-4
③ C100-2
④ H000-0 — RAW EDGE
⑤
⑥

Page | 140

101 Sewing Seams

Season:	SS22	Designer:	Peter
Collection:	Basics	Supplier:	PITU Tex
Range Size:	Unique	Delivery Date:	20/02/21
Proto Size:	- PROTOTYPE	Due Date:	02/03/21

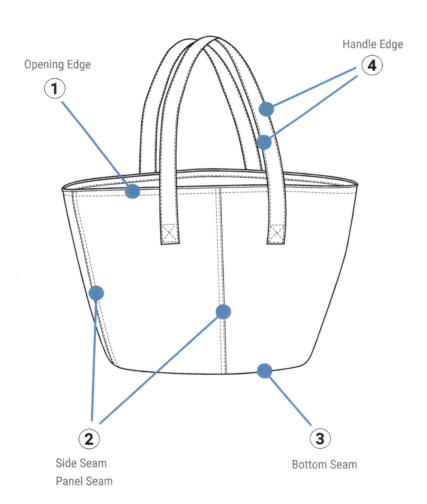

Handle Edge ④

Opening Edge ①

② Side Seam
Panel Seam

③ Bottom Seam

Thread:
nylon - nr.30
black
2 spc

INDEX

A

Abbreviations, 146

B

Band, Exposed, 74 to 77
Basic
  Seam, 27 to 29
  Topstitch, 115
  Topstitch with Flap, 115
Binded Edge, 64 to 66
Blind
  Hem, 61
  Stitch, 113
Boning Seam, 48
Bound(ed)
  Exposed Band, 76
  Exposed Piping, 84
  Exposed Tape, 80
  Hem, 67 to 69
  Seam, 37 to 39
Box
  Pleat, 104 to 107
  Inverted (Pleat), 106

C

Chain Stitch, 112
Construction Seams, 25 to 53
Cover Stitch, 113

D

Dart, 101
Details (seams), 95 to 107

E

Edge
  Stitch, 114
  Binded, 64 to 66
  Raw, 58
  Roll Stitch, 58
  Serged, 58
  Taped, 65
  Turned, 90 to 92
  Unhemmed, 57 to 59
Exposed
  Band, 74 to 77
  Piping, 82 to 85
  Tape, 78 to 81

F

Faced Hem, 70 to 73
Felled Seam, 30 to 33
Flat Seam, 32
Flatlock Stitch, 113
Fold Hem, 60 to 63
French Seam, 34 to 36

H

Hairline Seam, 28
Hem(s)
  and Finishes, 55 to 92
  Blind, 61
  Bound, 67 to 69
  Faced, 70 to 73
  Fold, 60 to 63

Rolled, 61
Sandwich, 86 to 89
Hong Kong Seam, 47

I
Inverted Box Pleat, 106
Icons, 147

L
Lapped Seam, 43 to 45

O
Open Seam, 46 to 49
Overlock Stitch, 112

P
Patch Seam, 97 to 99
Pin Tuck, 102
Piping, Exposed, 82 to 85
Plain Stitch, 112
Pleat, 100 to 103
  Box, 104 to 107
  Inverted Box, 106

R
Raw Edge, 58
Roll Stitch, 112
  Edge, 58
Rolled Hem, 61

S
Sandwich
  Hem, 86 to 89
  Seam, 50 to 53

Seam(s)
  Basic, 27 to 29
  Boning, 48
  Bound, 37 to 39
  Codes, 144, 145
  Construction, 25 to 53
  Felled, 30 to 33
  Flat, 32
  French, 34 to 36
  Hairline, 28
  Hong Kong, 47
  Lapped, 43 to 45
  Open, 46 to 49
  Sandwich, 50 to 53
  Welt, 40 to 42
Serged Edge, 58
Stitches, 112, 113

T
Tech Packs, 116 to 141
Topstitch, 114, 115
Tuck (Pin-Tuck), 102
Turned Edge, 90 to 92

U
Under-stitch, 114
Unhemmed Edge, 57 to 59

W
Welt Seam, 40 to 42

Z
Zig-Zag Stitch, 112

ABC Seams®

SEAM CODES | INDEX

C

C000-1, P.28
C000-1 (OS), P.28
C000-1 +SE, P.28

C010-1, P.35

C100-1, P.31
C100-1 (OS), P.31
C100-1 +SE, P.31
C100-2, P.31
C100-3, P.31
C100-3 (OS), P.31
C100-4, P.31
C100-4 (CS), P.31
C100-4 (FS), P.32

C101-9, P.38
C101-10, P.38
C101-12, P.38

C110-1, P.41
C110-1x, P.41
C110-2, P.41

C120-1, P.44
C120-4, P.44
C120-4 (CS), P.44

C200-1, P.47
C200-1 +SE, P.47
C200-2, P.47
C200-2 +SE, P.47

C201-9, P.47

C210-3, P.47

C220-2, P.48

CD190-1, P.51
CD190-2, P.51
CD190-4, P.51
CD190-5, P.51
CD190-8, P.51
CD190-9, P.51

D

D100-1, P.102

D110-0, P.101
D110-10, P.101
D110-13, P.101

D111-0, P.105
D111-0A, P.105
D111-1, P.105

D112-0A, P.106
D112-1, P.106
D112-5, P.106

D210-1, P.98
D210-2, P.98
D210-3, P.98
D210-4, P.98

H

H000-0, P.58
H000-0 +RS, P.58
H000-0 +SE, P.58

H100-0 +BS, P.61
H100-1 +SE, P.61
H100-2 (CS), P.61
H100-2 (FS), P.61

H101-9, P.68
H101-10, P.68
H101-12, P.68

H110-2, P.61
H110-10, P.61
H110-12, P.61

H120-0 +SE, P.62
H120-1 +SE, P.62
H120-2 (CS), P.62

H130-3, P.62
H130-6, P.62
H130-11, P.62

H140-11 +SE, P.71
H140-12 +SE, P.71

H150-31, P.71
H150-32, P.71
H150-45x, P.71

H160-0, P.91
H160-1, P.91
H160-4, P.91

H200-1, P.65
H200-3 (CS), P.65

H210-1 (OS), P.75
H210-1 + SE, P.75
H210-3, P.75
H210-4, P.75
H210-4 (CS), P.75
H210-4 (FS), P.75

H211-9, P.76

H310-1 (OS), P.79
H310-3, P.79
H310-3x, P.79
H310-4, P.79

H311-9, P.80

H400-1, P.83
H400-2, P.83
H400-3, P.83
H400-4, P.83

H401-9, P.84

HD190-1, P.87
HD190-10, P.87
HD190-2, P.87
HD190-4, P.87
HD190-5, P.87
HD190-8, P.87

ABBREVIATIONS

Stitches

BS	Blind Stitch
CS	Cover Stitch
FS	Flatlock Stitch
OS	Overlock Stitch
RS	Roll Stitch
SA	Seam Allowance
SE	Serged Edge

General

AQL	Acceptable Quality Level
BOM	Bill of Materials
CB	Center Back
CF	Center Front
CMT	Cut, Make and Trim
FOB	Freight on Board
HSP	Highest Shoulder Point
POM	Point of Measure
PPS	Pre-Production Sample
QMS	Quality Management System
SPC	Stitches per Centimeter
SPI	Stitches per Inches
SS	Salesman Sample

ICONS

K knit fabric

⭐ the most used

🌿 the most durable

💎 high-end

$ the lowest cost

♥ favorite

📷 photograpy

ABOUT ABC SEAMS

A good understanding of seams is crucial to achieving your goals as a designer or product developer.
Any information, feedback or explanation between you and your team (internal and external) needs to be clear and precise. This is crucial to avoid confusion or misunderstanding.

Our purpose is to help you to *communicate your designs in a simple and effective way*.
To do this, we have developed a standardized sewing seam language that allows you to select, name, and look up any kind of seam. In this way, anyone, at anytime, anywhere in the world can know exactly what kind of construction you have requested.

Using this tool has other benefits, for example:
- make better decisions
- reduce the development time
- be more creative

Fin more info on our website: *www.abcseams.com*

ACKNOWLEDGMENTS

To our contributors, thank you for the invaluable feedback, advice, support, and for sharing your experience in this book:

Belén Asensio,

Clara Serenellini,

Elisenda Vidella,

Eva Basagaña Rusiñol,

Gabriela Bondancia,

Jaime García Sánchez,

Jane Cruise,

Julieta Bernadó,

Karen Ruiz,

Mina Park,

Rocío Rapisarda,

Sally Brown,

Gabby BR,

Izarra González,

Mercedes Sogo,

Mila Moura,

Robert Cooper,

Lisa, Billy, and Stella.

Picture Credits

Page 17: **Joshua Rawson Harris**

Page 73: **Brooke Cagle**

Page 77: **Jonnelle Yankovich**

Page 81: **Houcine Ncib**

Page 85: **Kal Visuals**

Page 93: **Alex Perez**

Page 103: **Liz Weddon**

Page 107: **Sahin Yesilyaprak**

CPSIA information can be obtained
at www.ICGtesting.com
Printed in the USA
LVHW070331100822
725602LV00008B/148